FRED McGRIFF

BEN GRIEVE

QUINTON McCRACKEN

ROLANDO ARROJO

GREG VAUGHN

ALBIE LOPEZ

BOBBY SMITH

ESTEBAN YAN

JOSE CANSECO

VINNY CASTILLA

WADE BOGGS

WILSON ALVAREZ

THE HISTORY OF THE
TAMPA BAY
DEVIL RAYS

JOHN NICHOLS

CREATIVE C EDUCATION

Published by Creative Education, 123 South Broad Street, Mankato, MN 56001

Creative Education is an imprint of The Creative Company.

Designed by Rita Marshall.

Photographs by AllSport (Al Bello, Stephen Dunn, Jed Jacobsohn, Danny Moloshok, David Seelig,

Rick Stewart, Peter J. Taylor), Associated Press/Wide World Photos, Icon Sports Media (John Cordes,

Chuck Solomon), Sports Gallery (Al Messerschmidt), SportsChrome (Rob Tringali Jr., Michael Zito)

Library of Congress Cataloging-in-Publication Data

Nichols, John, 1966- The history of the Tampa Bay Devil Rays / by John Nichols.

p. cm. — (Baseball)   ISBN 1-58341-225-5

Summary: Highlights the new major league baseball franchise that began play in Tampa Bay,

Florida, in 1998.

1. Tampa Bay Devil Rays (Baseball team)—History—

Juvenile literature. [1. Tampa Bay Devil Rays (Baseball team)—History.

2. Baseball—History.] I. Title. II. Baseball (Mankato, Minn.).

GV875.T26 N53 2002   796.357'64—dc21   2001047876

First Edition 9 8 7 6 5 4 3 2 1

WHEN THE

SUN SETS ON THE BEAUTIFUL BAY WATERS OF TAMPA,

Florida, nature's richest colors come out to play. Crystal shades of

green, blue, purple, and black dance on the horizon of the Gulf of

Mexico, while the city's skyline shimmers in the fading light. Tampa

and its neighboring city, St. Petersburg, are blessed with a beautiful

5

climate that attracts visitors from all over the world.

Although warm weather and tropical beauty are probably

Tampa's biggest draws, the city is also home to many other attrac-

tions. Since 1998, one of the most popular of these has been the

city's major league baseball team—the Tampa Bay Devil Rays.

Named after a large, unusual-looking fish native to the area, the

Devil Rays quickly hooked Tampa's sports fans.

ROLANDO ARROJO

{BASEBALL COMES TO TAMPA} Although the Devil Rays

didn't begin play until 1998, the Tampa-St. Petersburg area was no

In a **1914** stranger to big-league baseball. The two cities had

exhibition,

the Chicago been a spring training home to 14 different major-

Cubs and St.

Louis Browns league teams since 1913. For decades, big-league clubs

played the

first pro game arrived each year in late February and March, spent

in Tampa. several weeks there getting into shape, and then

6 headed back to their northern homes.

Finally, in March 1995, major league baseball decided to place

expansion teams in two new cities: Tampa and Phoenix, Arizona.

The Devil Rays were placed in the American League's (AL) Eastern

Division, where they would compete against such traditional

powerhouses as the New York Yankees and Boston Red Sox. "We

are excited about building rivalries with some of baseball's oldest

and most respected franchises," said Devil Rays owner Vincent

BEN GRIEVE

The "Crime Dog," Fred McGriff, led Tampa Bay in RBI in the team's first three seasons.

FRED McGRIFF

Naimoli. "We can't wait to get started."

One of Naimoli's first tasks was to find a home for his team. Fortunately, Tampa already had a large domed stadium ready for action. Originally known as the Florida Suncoast Dome, the stadium was built in the late 1980s to help the city attract a big-league team. In the early '90s, the stadium was renamed the Thunderdome when it served as the home of the National Hockey League's Tampa Bay Lightning. When major league baseball came to Tampa, the stadium underwent an $85-million facelift and was renamed Tropicana Field.

The new park featured many nostalgic features. The "Trop," as it was soon dubbed, had outfield dimensions roughly the same as those of Ebbets Field, the irregular but beloved home of the old Brooklyn Dodgers. It also featured a unique modern touch. After

In **1997**, the Devil Rays used the top pick in the expansion draft to take hurler Tony Saunders.

9

TONY SAUNDERS

Though the team's wins have been few, Tampa Bay has featured some strong pitching.

JUAN GUZMAN

Devil Rays victories, the stadium's translucent roof was lit bright
orange, a color symbolic of Tropicana Dole Beverages, the

ballpark's sponsor.

{DEVIL RAYS DEBUT} The first edition of the
Tampa Bay Devil Rays was a team short on stars and
long on untested players and aging veterans. Despite
its lack of depth, manager Larry Rothschild's roster

12 did feature two big names: first baseman Fred McGriff and third
baseman Wade Boggs.

McGriff and Boggs, both Tampa natives, had come home after
long and brilliant careers elsewhere. McGriff had spent 11 big-league
seasons with the Toronto Blue Jays, San Diego Padres, and Atlanta
Braves before coming to Tampa Bay in a trade with the Braves. The
6-foot-3 and 215-pound left-handed slugger had long been one of
baseball's most consistent run producers. Each year from 1988 to

WADE BOGGS

1994, McGriff hit 30 or more home runs and drove in at least 80

runs. Known as the "Crime Dog," McGriff gave the Devil Rays'

lineup some bite.

The 39-year-old Boggs came to Tampa Bay to finish a stellar

career that had begun in 1982 with the Boston Red Sox. His sweet

left-handed stroke had produced an amazing .331 career batting average and five AL batting titles. A two-time Gold Glove award winner, Boggs also was a solid defensive presence. "Wade and Fred are here to show our young guys what it takes to be a winner in this league," noted Rothschild. "All these kids will be better for playing with them."

McGriff and Boggs helped the Devil Rays get off to a solid start in 1998. Tampa Bay finished April with a record of 12–13, the best ever in that month by a first-year expansion team. However, as the season wore on, wins came less frequently. Despite solid contributions from outfielder Quinton McCracken and pitcher Rolando Arrojo, the Devil Rays fell into last place in the AL East and stayed there, finishing the season with a 63–99 mark.

{ADDING SOME THUNDER} Even though the Devil Rays finished in last place in 1998, there was much to like about the team. Despite having an extremely young pitching staff, Tampa Bay—led

In **1998**, Tampa Bay swept a four-game series against a strong Orioles team in Baltimore.

14

QⁱⁱINTON McᶜRACKEN

by Arrojo and youngsters Albie Lopez and Jim Mecir—posted the

fourth-best ERA in the league (4.35). The team was also very sound

defensively, making only 94 errors, second-fewest in the majors.

What the team lacked was offensive punch. Knowing that

McGriff was the only established power threat, opposing teams

rarely gave the veteran slugger good pitches to hit. Young hitters such as third baseman Bobby Smith and outfielders Bubba Trammell and Randy Winn did their best to pick up the slack, but going into 1999, the Devil Rays knew they needed to add some thunder to their lineup.

Before the start of the season, Tampa Bay signed free agent slugger Jose Canseco. The 34-year-old outfielder/designated hitter had been one of the game's biggest stars while with the Oakland Athletics in the late 1980s and early '90s. The 6-foot-4 and 245-pounder won the AL's Most Valuable Player (MVP) award in 1988 when he became the first player ever to hit 40 home runs and steal 40 bases in the same season.

During the mid-1990s, Canseco suffered a series of injuries that limited him to duty as a designated hitter. Still, the hulking native of Havana, Cuba, retained his reputation as one of baseball's

Rookie Bobby Smith showed great promise at the plate in **1998**, recording two four-hit games.

BOBBY SMITH

Infielder Aubrey Huff showed star potential in Tampa Bay's minor-league system.

most feared hitters. "With Jose hitting behind Fred, it gives us a left-right combination in the middle of our lineup that will be tough," McCracken noted. "All I'll have to do is get on base and let the big guys drive me in."

McCracken was right about the damage Canseco and McGriff would wreak upon AL pitching. In 1999, McGriff hit .310, slammed 32 home runs, and racked up

104 RBI, while Canseco hit .279, belted 34 homers, and drove in 95 runs. The only problem for the Devil Rays was that the slugging duo appeared in only 98 games together. Canseco was sidelined for a month and a half with a back injury, and without him, the Devil Rays struggled mightily. With Canseco and McGriff in the lineup together, Tampa Bay's record was a respectable 45–53. But during games that Canseco spent on the disabled list, the Devil Rays went a paltry 24–40.

Strapping slugger Jose Canseco got off to a fast start in **1999**, hitting 10 home runs in April.

JOSE CANSECO

Canseco's back problem was just one in a long list of injuries

that plagued Tampa Bay in 1999. The Devil Rays put 18 players on

the disabled list—the most in the major leagues—yet still managed

to post a 69–93 record. Along with the increase in victories, one of

the major highlights of the Devil Rays' season came when Wade

Boggs crunched a home run for his 3,000th career hit. The feat made Boggs only the 23rd player in big-league history to reach the 3,000-hit milestone. After the season, Boggs retired. The following

April, the Devil Rays retired his number 12 jersey, the first number to be so honored by the team.

{ACHES AND PAINS} Heading into the 2000 season, the Devil Rays continued to search for answers to their losing ways. In the free agent market, the team landed slugger Greg Vaughn from the Cincinnati Reds and speedy outfielder Gerald Williams from the Atlanta Braves. The team was also beginning to reap talent from its own minor-league system. Home-grown pitchers Bryan Rekar and Ryan Rupe each showed promise during 1999 stints with the team and were counted on to bolster the starting rotation.

Tampa Bay also made a key trade with the Colorado Rockies for third baseman Vinny Castilla. The 33-year-old Castilla had been

ROBE TO E N N EZ

Power hitter Vinny Castilla was brought in to beef up Tampa Bay's offense in **2000**.

VINNY CASTILLA

extremely productive while playing in the mile-high air of Colorado—averaging 38 homers and 112 RBI a season from 1995 to 1999—and with Boggs's retirement, the Devil Rays were in need of a strong bat.

With a restocked lineup and a promising young pitching staff in the making, the Devil Rays had high hopes in 2000. Unfortunately, injuries hit hard again. Before the season even got underway, top starter Wilson Alvarez was lost for the year with a shoulder injury. One week into the season, number-two starter Juan Guzman also suffered a season-ending shoulder injury.

Despite the devastating losses on its pitching staff, Tampa Bay reached the end of June with a decent 32–45 record. Then disaster struck. The Devil Rays lost Castilla, Canseco, Vaughn, and Williams to a series of injuries that kept the heart of the lineup off

WILSON ALVAREZ

the field for nearly a month. "In baseball, we make our own luck,

but to get this many injuries to so many key guys is amazing,"

said Fred McGriff. "I have to say our luck's been awful."

Although stripped of most of their weapons, the Devil Rays

refused to give up. Led by hard-throwing pitcher Albie Lopez,

Tampa Bay stayed afloat in July by going 12–14. By August, Williams and Vaughn returned to the lineup and gave Tampa Bay a much-needed lift. For the season, Williams belted 21 homers and drove in 89 runs as the leadoff hitter, while Vaughn chipped in 28 homers and 74 RBI in only 127 games.

Castilla and Canseco's injury woes turned out to be the biggest disappointments of the season. Castilla never found a rhythm while enduring three long stretches on the disabled list, and Canseco's back and heel injuries kept him out of the lineup so much that the team waived him late in the season. With all the injuries and turmoil, the Devil Rays finished the season 69–92.

In one **2000** game, Greg Vaughn and the Rays battled the Orioles for a club-record 15 innings.

27

{YOUTH IS SERVED IN TAMPA} The Devil Rays' 2000 season was a disappointment, but they did get some eye-opening performances from players who were expected to be a major part of the team's future. Infielder Aubrey Huff and outfielder/first baseman

GREG VAUGHN

Steve Cox both took advantage of midseason call-ups from the minors to cement starting jobs with the Devil Rays.

Gerald Williams hit the very first pitch of the **2000** season for a home run (against the Twins).

Huff stepped in for Castilla at third base and responded with a solid .287 average, while Cox put together a .283 average with 11 homers in only 116 games. The team's pitchers also appeared to be on the right track, as Rekar and Rupe, along with hard-throwing right-hander Esteban Yan, gained valuable experience.

In an effort to add more young talent before the 2001 season, the Devil Rays traded closer Roberto Hernandez and pitcher Cory Lidle to the Oakland A's for outfielder Ben Grieve. The 6-foot-4 and 230-pound Grieve had burst upon the scene in 1998, winning the AL Rookie of the Year award. With one of the prettiest swings in baseball, Grieve seemed destined for superstardom. But in the two seasons after his rookie year, his average dipped, and the A's decided

GERALD WILLIAMS

to make the trade. "We feel that Ben still has a great future ahead of him," noted Devil Rays general manager Chuck LaMar. "He's only 25 years old, but he's averaged 25 homers and 90 RBI in his first three big-league seasons. We needed some good young talent, and we think Ben fits the bill perfectly."

Tampa Bay's 2001 decision to bring in new blood also resulted in the firing of manager Larry Rothschild. Rothschild was soon replaced by Hal McRae. McRae, a star player for the Cincinnati Reds and Kansas City Royals in the 1970s and '80s, quickly decided to go with the team's younger talents. Veterans Vinny Castilla and Gerald Williams were released at the beginning of the year, Fred McGriff was traded away at midseason, and promising prospects such as outfielder Jason Tyner and infielder Damian Rolls were given every opportunity to earn starting roles.

Outfielder Randy Winn legged out six triples in **2001**, tops among all Tampa Bay hitters.

RANDY WINN

First baseman
Steve Cox
was part of
a promising
lineup that
took the field
in **2002**.

STEVE COX

Tampa Bay pitchers appreciated the sure glove of young infielder Damian Rolls.

DAMIAN ROLLS

With their emphasis on youth, the Devil Rays face taking steps backward before moving forward. Tampa Bay has learned that the road from expansion team to pennant contender is a challenging one. But in spite of the many ups and downs, Tampa's baseball-crazy fans keep hope alive for a better day. With a little luck and some patience, the time will soon come when the Devil Rays swim in the warm waters of success.

A keen-eyed hitter, catcher Toby Hall was expected to play a major role in the team's future.

TOBY HALL